All About Ame

AMERICAN INDIANS

Paul Robert Walker

KINGFISHER
NEW YORK

All About America: AMERICAN INDIANS
All rights reserved. No part of this book may be reproduced or utilized in any form or by any means, electronic or mechanical, including photocopying, recording, or by any information storage or retrieval systems, without permission in writing from the publisher.

LONDON & NEW YORK

Published in the United States by Kingfisher,
175 Fifth Ave., New York, NY 10010
Kingfisher is an imprint of Macmillan Children's Books, London.
All rights reserved.

Distributed in the U.S. by Macmillan, 175 Fifth Ave.,
New York, NY 10010

Library of Congress Cataloging-in-Publication data has been applied for.

ISBN paperback 978-0-7534-6517-2
ISBN reinforced library binding 978-0-7534-6694-0

Kingfisher books are available for special promotions and premiums. For details contact: Special Markets Department, Macmillan, 175 Fifth Ave., New York, NY 10010.

For more information, please visit www.kingfisherbooks.com

Printed in China
10 9 8 7 6 5 4 3 2 1
1TR/0811/UNTD/WKT/140MA

The All About America series was produced for Kingfisher by Bender Richardson White, Uxbridge, U.K.
Editor: Lionel Bender
Designer: Ben White
DTP: Neil Sutton
Production: Kim Richardson
Consultant: Richard Jensen, Research Professor of History, Culver Stockton College, Missouri

Sources of quotations and excerpts
Page 11, Catlin quote: Catlin, George. *Letters and Notes on the Manners, Customs, and Conditions of North American Indians.* Letter No. 11, Mandan Village, Upper Missouri. First published in London, 1884. See: http://www.xmission.com/~drudy/mtman/html/catlin/index.html (October, 2010)
Page 21, desert reference: *The New Encyclopedia of the American West*, ed. Howard R. Lamar. New Haven, CT: Yale University Press, 1998, under the heading "Great American Desert."
Page 25, hostile reference: Utley, Robert. *The Lance and the Shield: The Life and Times of Sitting Bull*, page 127. New York: Henry Holt and Company, 1993.
Page 26, Sitting Bull song: Utley, Robert. *The Lance and the Shield: The Life and Times of Sitting Bull*, page 233. New York: Henry Holt and Company, 1993.
Page 28, Wovoka quote: Hittman, Michael. *Wovoka and the Ghost Dance*, page 8. Yerington, NV: Yerington Paiute Tribe; Carson City, NV: Grace Dangberg Foundation, 1990.

Acknowledgments
The publishers would like to thank the following illustrators for their contribution to this book: Mark Bergin, Peter Dennis, James Field, Terry Gabbey, Nick Hewetson, John James, Malcolm McGregor, and Gerald Wood. Map: Neil Sutton.
Book cover design: Mike Davis and Neal Cobourne.
Cover artwork: Mark Bergin and Terry Gabbey.
The publishers thank the following for supplying photos for this book: b = bottom, c = center, l = left, t = top, m = middle:
© The Art Archive: pages 29b (The Kobal Collection) • Breslich and Foss: pages 10tl; 10–11bc; 18–19tc; 23r •
© The Bridgeman Art Library: page 15b (© Heini Schneebeli); 26–27bc (Museum of the North American Indian, New York); 29tl (Peter Newark American Pictures) • Dorling Kindersley: page 23b (© Geoff Brightling) •
© Getty Images: page 8–9c (Nativestock.com/Marilyn Angel Wynn); 12bl • © The Granger Collection/TopFoto pages 4tl; 4–5tc; 5t; 6m; 7m; 7b; 8tl; 8bl; 10tr; 10b; 12tl; 12tr; 12–13c; 14m; 15tr; 16tr; 17m; 17tr; 20tl; 20b; 21tl; 22tr; 22b; 24ml; 24mr; 25t; 25br; 26mr; 27t; 28m; 28b • istockphoto.com: pages 4ml (© Steve Shepard); 16–17cl (© Mark Goddard); 16–17cr (© Gabor Kecskemeti); 29m (© Janice McBride) • Library of Congress: page 1c (pnp/ppmsca.15975); 1, 2–3, 30–31, 32 (pnp/ppmsc.02512); 13tr (pnp/cph.3b05011); 19t (pnp/ppmsc.02512); 22m (pnp/ppmsca.15976); 28tl (pnp-ppmsc.02552); 29tr (pnp-npcc.20304)
Every effort has been made to trace the copyright holders of the images. The publishers apologize for any omissions.

Note to readers: The website addresses listed in this book are correct at the time of publishing. However, due to the ever-changing nature of the Internet, website addresses and content can change. Websites can contain links that are unsuitable for children. The publisher cannot be held responsible for changes in website addresses or content or for information obtained through third-party websites. We strongly advise that Internet searches should be supervised by an adult.

CONTENTS

Introduction

American Indians looks at the lives of the first peoples to have settled in North America and how their customs and traditions were dramatically changed following the arrival of Europeans in the 1500s. It describes and illustrates American Indians' homes, clothes, weapons, lifestyles, and their interactions with white settlers mainly from around 1600 to 1900. The story is presented as a series of double-page articles, each one looking at a particular topic. It is illustrated with paintings, engravings, and photographs from the time, mixed with artists' impressions of everyday scenes and situations.

A Continent of Peoples

Early American Indian cultures

The first prehistoric American Indians were hunters and gatherers who traveled in small groups. Later, with skills to use natural resources and the development of farming, these people could stay in one place, and large settlements began to form.

Scholars debate when American Indian people first arrived in North America. They probably reached Alaska from Asia around 16,500 years ago. Spear points found near modern-day Clovis, New Mexico, indicate that Indians were hunting Ice-Age animals such as mastodons around 11,000 to 13,000 years ago.

The Clovis hunters gradually spread throughout what is now the United States and gave rise to many different cultures. In the Ohio River valley, two similar cultures—the Adena and the Hopewell—developed from 1000 B.C. to A.D. 700. They are called the Mound Builders because they built large mounds of earth to bury their dead. The mounds took years to build and indicate that these people had a large, complex society with rulers and workers.

▶ **Limestone figure of a kneeling man, from the Mississippian settlement at Shiloh, Tennessee, around A.D. 1450**

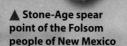

▲ **Stone-Age spear point of the Folsom people of New Mexico**

Anasazi Cliff Houses
In the Southwest, an ancient people called the Anasazi built multistory dwellings similar to modern apartments out of adobe and rocks. They were sometimes built below cliffs for protection, like the one above in Mesa Verde National Park.

▶ **At its height, from A.D. 1050 to 1200, Cahokia had a population of between 10,000 and 20,000—more than London, England, at the time. By 1400, Cahokia had been abandoned.**

Temple Mounds
After the Adena and the Hopewell people came a more sophisticated culture. This is called the Mississippian, because the people lived in the Mississippi River valley. They built large earthen mounds with temples at the top. Priests, rulers, and warriors lived on the mounds while the common people lived below.

How Do We Know?

American Indians left no written records of their cultures, so most of what we know comes from archaeology—the study of old objects, structures, skeletons, weapons, clothing, trade goods, and other remains. Early explorers also wrote down oral stories told by the Indians they encountered and recorded the life they saw in words, paintings, drawings, and photographs.

Serpent Mound

The Great Serpent Mound in southwestern Ohio is about 3 feet (1 m) high and stretches 1,330 feet (400 m). In an aerial photograph (like the one above), it looks like a giant uncoiling snake swallowing an egg. Archaeologists think it was built around A.D. 1000 but are not sure by whom.

Indian Map

When Europeans first arrived in the 1500s, there were hundreds of Indian tribes in North America. The map below shows how we are organizing the tribes in this book, by geographical region.

NORTHWESTERN

CALIFORNIAN

PLAINS

EASTERN WOODLAND

N

SOUTHEASTERN

SOUTHWESTERN

Religion and trade

The two largest American Indian cities of early North America were Cahokia in present-day Illinois and Chaco in present-day New Mexico. Within Chaco, the greatest city of the Anasazi culture, were several "great houses" built of sandstone and wood. The largest of these, Pueblo Bonito, contains about 800 rooms. (See a pueblo on page 13.)

Evidence suggests that both cities were the centers of trade and religion for the surrounding areas. Many of the rooms at Chaco were used for storage or as guest rooms when people came for special spiritual events. Both cities and their cultures began to decline around A.D. 1200, when the climate changed and a drought came to North America. The cities were empty when the first Europeans arrived.

Eastern Woodland Tribes

Algonquin- and Iroquois-speaking peoples

American Indians of the Eastern Woodlands thrived on the resources of the forests. They used the trees, wild plants, and wild animals for shelter, food, and clothing. They also developed farming and fishing and lived in villages for as long as the forests could support them.

The Eastern Woodland Indians lived in all of what is now the northeastern United States. Almost all of these tribes spoke a form of either the Algonquin or the Iroquois language. Because they had rich natural resources and lived in villages for several years at a time, they developed complex societies. They even had groups of tribes—called confederacies, leagues, or nations—that agreed to keep peace with one another and fight their common enemies.

The most powerful Indian nation was the Iroquois Confederacy, with six tribes living in what is now New York State and northern Pennsylvania. Others were the Abnaki Confederacy in Maine and the Powhatan Confederacy in eastern Virginia. Powerful individual tribes were the Shawnee of present-day Tennessee and the Ottawa and Pottawatomi of Michigan.

▲ An Eastern Woodland warrior with a wooden fighting club

The Powhatan Confederacy

The Powhatans and other tribes in the coastal Virginia area built their homes, called *yehakins*, by bending young trees (saplings) and covering them with bark or mats woven with reeds. Powhatan was the name of one small village whose chief, also called Powhatan, controlled 32 tribes in the early 1600s.

▶ Chief Powhatan is shown sitting on a throne in this engraving from a 1624 book by English colonial leader John Smith.

◀ As in most Eastern Woodland tribes, the Powhatan men were hunters, fishermen, and warriors. The women tended the crops, gathered wild plants, cooked, made clothes, and took care of the children.

6

The Iroquois Longhouse

The Iroquois and some other northeastern tribes lived in longhouses made of strong saplings bent and connected by other saplings. The structure was then covered with bark, overlapping like shingles on a modern house. Many related families lived together in each longhouse, which could be 40 to 200 feet (12 to 60 m) long.

▲ Village life among the Iroquois, from a French engraving, 1664

Law and order

According to Iroquois legend, two leaders, Deganawida and Hiawatha, traveled among the northeastern tribes and persuaded many of them to follow the Great Law of Peace. The result of this effort was the Iroquois League, later called the Iroquois Confederacy when the Iroquois organized to fight white European settlers. At first there were five tribes who lived in what is now upstate New York: the Mohawk, Oneida, Onondaga, Cayuga, and Seneca. Later, in 1722, a sixth tribe called the Tuscarora joined them, and they are still known today as the Six Nations.

Woodland religion

Like most American Indians, Eastern Woodland people saw themselves as part of a natural world with a spirit in every living thing. For the Iroquois, the Great Spirit was Orenda, and the Flying Head was an evil spirit that could be battled by the False Face Society.

◄ This False Face mask is typical of masks used in rituals by the Iroquois False Face Society.

Southeastern Tribes
Cherokee, Seminole, and Natchez peoples

Like Indians of the Eastern Woodlands, the people of the Southeast had a lot of rainfall and natural resources. But their land was warmer and wetter, with swamps in places. Their forests were thick and humid, similar to jungles.

The Southeastern culture area stretches from the Atlantic Ocean to present-day eastern Texas, and from the Gulf of Mexico into Tennessee, the Carolinas, and western Virginia.

The largest tribe of the area was the Cherokee, who spoke an Iroquois language and lived mainly in what is now Georgia and the Carolinas. The Southeastern tribes lived by farming, hunting, fishing, and gathering. In most areas of the South, the soil is sandier than in the North. This kind of soil loses its fertility more quickly, so Southeastern tribes moved their villages more often to find rich soil. Villages were usually built in river valleys, and rivers served as transportation routes.

Some Southeastern tribes kept slaves, first capturing other Indians and later buying black slaves from white owners.

▲ A Seminole woman and child, photographed around 1905

▼ A Seminole village of houses on stilts called *chikees*. The open sides and raised floor let air flow through and also prevented flooding in heavy rains.

▶ The Natchez had a social system that included nobles, workers, and slaves. After rebelling against the French in 1729, they were destroyed as a tribe, but survivors lived among other Southeastern tribes.

▲ Seminole war leader Osceola, painted by artist George Catlin in 1838

Seminole
The Seminole tribe developed when Creek Indians left Georgia in the early 1700s and moved into Florida. They became a powerful tribe who fought the United States in three separate wars during the early 19th century. They lost and were removed to reservations in Oklahoma, where they live now.

Natchez
The Natchez tribe lived around the present-day city of Natchez, Mississippi. Unlike other Southeastern tribes, they continued to practice the religion of the Cahokia Mound Builders, including worshiping a godlike leader called the Great Sun and making human sacrifices.

▼ Natchez village slaves, called stinkards, carried their leader, known as the Great Sun, between the temple mounds and homes.

Cherokee
When Europeans arrived, the Cherokee controlled large areas of land in the southern Appalachian Mountains, including parts of eight present-day states. Like the Iroquois, whose language they share, the Cherokee had a sophisticated society, culture, and religion. Today, they are the largest American Indian tribe, with 730,000 people claiming Cherokee blood.

◄ Cherokee baskets made from woven twigs and stems

The three sisters
For the Southeastern tribes, as with many North American Indians, the most important crops were maize (corn), beans, and squash. The Indians called these the three sisters. When planted together, they help one another grow. The maize stalks give the beans a structure to climb; the beans provide nitrogen that the other plants take from the soil; and the squash covers the ground, helping prevent weeds. The three sisters contain different nutrients, so when they are eaten together they provide a balanced diet.

Because of the longer growing season in the South, the Southeastern tribes could often survive on their crops and on the wild fruits and vegetables they gathered. They did hunt and fish, but meat was not a large part of their diet. Their favorite meat was bear, and bear fat was used for many purposes, including making a corn cake similar to the cornbread we eat today.

The Plains Tribes

Life before the introduction of horses

Most people think of American Indians as living in tepees and hunting buffalo. The Plains Indians did these things, but their nomadic way of life did not develop fully until horses were brought to North America by the Spanish.

The Plains Indians lived on the vast grasslands that extend from the Mississippi River to the Rocky Mountains and from central Canada into southern Texas. Tens of millions of buffalo once grazed in this region. Toward the east are tall grasses—called the prairie—where there is enough rainfall for farming. Farther west are the short grasses of the Great Plains, which are drier and higher in elevation.

Before the Europeans arrived, most Plains Indian tribes lived in permanent villages on the prairie, in homes that were usually made of wood and earth. They farmed, gathered wild plants, and hunted small animals. In the fall or spring, they left their villages to hunt buffalo, living in tepees that could be moved as they followed the herds.

◀ Arrows with feathers and stone tips

▲ A Dakota Sioux woman and Assiniboine girl. The tribes were enemies, so the girl may have been a captive.

Indian Warfare

Indian tribes fought one another to gain territory, to take captives, to avenge the death of a tribesman, to prove manhood, and to gain honor. For the Plains Indians, touching the enemy with a curved stick called a coup stick (see illustration on page 23) gained more honor than killing the enemy. Taking a scalp also gained honor and was celebrated with a special dance (below).

▶ A shield made of thick buffalo hide. The symbols on the shield were believed to give protection in battle.

▶ A scalp dance of the Lakota Sioux, as painted in 1850

10

Mandan Lodge

The Mandan lived in lodges made of earth and supported by large posts in the center. Painter George Catlin, who visited in 1833, wrote: "One is surprised when he [or she] enters them, to see the neatness, comfort, and spacious dimensions of these earth-covered dwellings."

Life without horses

Before the Spanish invaded Mexico in 1519, there were no horses in North or South America. (A larger North American horse died out or was hunted to extinction about 10,000 years previously.) The Indians of the southwestern plains first obtained Spanish horses around 1650, and the horse culture gradually expanded throughout the plains over the next 125 years.

▼ Before they had horses, the Plains Indians used large dogs to carry their tepees and other belongings when they went on hunting expeditions.

Southwestern Tribes
Pueblo, Hopi, Navajo, Apache, and Pima

The Southwestern peoples lived in an area of sunshine and little rain in lowland deserts. They adapted well to the land and climate and developed strong tribal cultures.

Aztec warrior

The Southwestern culture area covers most of New Mexico, Arizona, and western Texas and stretches far into Mexico. It was once the home of prehistoric hunters, and it later gave birth to great civilizations. The Pueblo and Hopi peoples are descendants of the Anasazi—also known as Ancestral Puebloans—while the Pima people descend from a desert culture called the Hohokam. Although the Navajo and Apache claim different origins, evidence suggests that they both came down from the north during the 1400s and that pressure from their raids may have contributed to the collapse of the Anasazi and Hohokam.

From Farther South

American Indian civilizations of Mexico and Central America developed earlier than those in what is now the United States and Canada. Among them were the Olmec, Maya, Toltec, and Aztec. They introduced farming and pottery to the peoples of the Southwest. Their cultures were larger and more sophisticated than those of the Mississippian, Hohokam, or Anasazi.

Established settlements

As they have done for centuries, and as the first European explorers found, the Pueblo live in villages in New Mexico, the Hopi live on mesas in northern Arizona, and the Pima live in the desert near present-day Phoenix.

▲ A Hopi man with a hoe, in his cornfield. Unlike most Southwestern Indian tribes, Hopi and Pueblo men worked as farmers.

▼ The hairstyle of these Hopi girls meant they had learned to grind corn and were ready for marriage.

▶ This clay bowl—in a style called Jeddito Yellow Ware—was found on one of the Hopi mesas and probably dates from around 1300 to 1450.

Living in towns and hilltop villages

The Pueblo and Hopi are both traditionally peaceful people who relied heavily on farming for their livelihood. The Pueblo were never a single tribe but rather a group of people who lived in towns with adobe and stone buildings, some with several stories and many rooms. (*Pueblo* is the Spanish word for town.) They spoke one of three completely different languages, and each town was a separate political unit.

The Hopi are related to the Pueblo in their culture and ancestry but speak yet another language. They lived—and still live—in villages on three flat-topped mountains, called mesas, in Arizona.

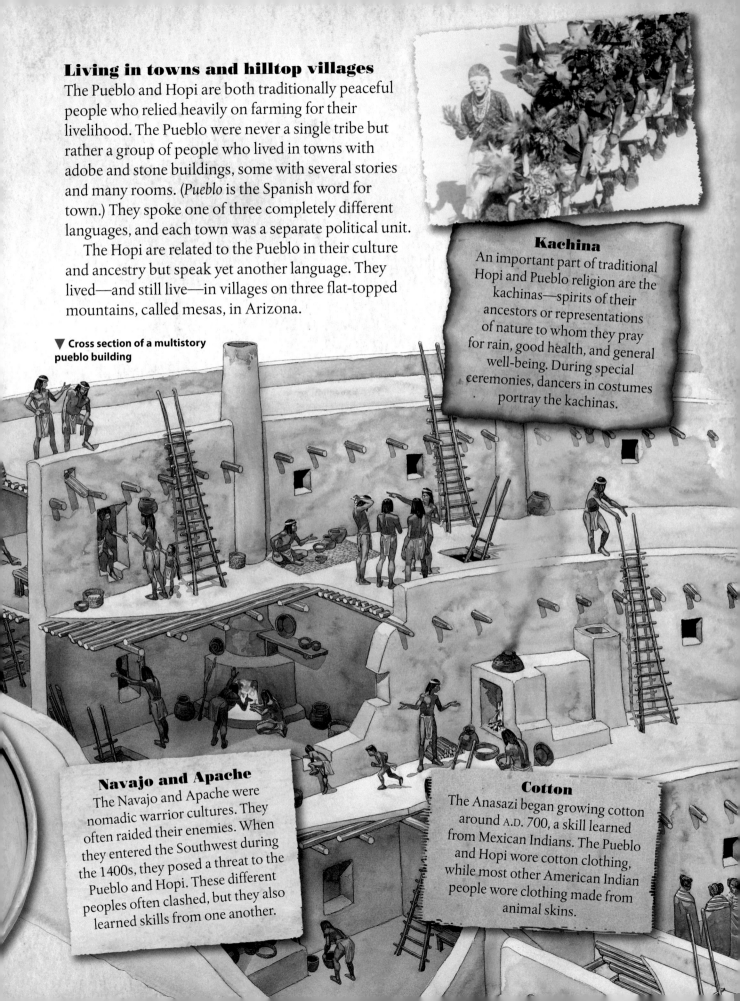

▼ **Cross section of a multistory pueblo building**

Kachina

An important part of traditional Hopi and Pueblo religion are the kachinas—spirits of their ancestors or representations of nature to whom they pray for rain, good health, and general well-being. During special ceremonies, dancers in costumes portray the kachinas.

Navajo and Apache

The Navajo and Apache were nomadic warrior cultures. They often raided their enemies. When they entered the Southwest during the 1400s, they posed a threat to the Pueblo and Hopi. These different peoples often clashed, but they also learned skills from one another.

Cotton

The Anasazi began growing cotton around A.D. 700, a skill learned from Mexican Indians. The Pueblo and Hopi wore cotton clothing, while most other American Indian people wore clothing made from animal skins.

Western Tribes
Living between mountains and the coast

There were four Western culture areas: the Great Basin in what is now eastern Colorado, Utah, and Nevada; the Columbia Plateau of Idaho, eastern Oregon, and Washington; California; and the Pacific Northwest.

American Indians west of the Rocky Mountains had more varied cultures than those in any other geographical region. Uniquely, very few of these tribes developed farming. The Great Basin people struggled to survive in a desert land, hunting small animals and digging for roots. Farther north, the Indians of the Columbia Plateau had rivers to provide salmon and other foods. The California Indians lived in a land with a mild climate where acorns were their principle food. In the Pacific Northwest, the people had such rich resources from the ocean, rivers, and forests that they developed a highly sophisticated culture.

▲ Haida man in raven mask

◄ The figure at the top of the totem pole is the thunderbird, a good spirit in Haida mythology as well as in the mythology of many other tribes.

▼ A Haida village on the Pacific Northwest coast, with canoes, wooden houses, and totem poles

Giving Away Wealth

Northwest Indians such as the Haida lived in wooden houses, carved big canoes and beautiful totem poles, and had all the food they needed from salmon and wild plants. They celebrated their wealth by giving it away in a ritual called the potlatch. This included feasting, dancing, and storytelling. The more a family could give away, the higher their social standing.

California Pomo

The Pomo lived in the hills and valleys north of present-day San Francisco. Like most California Indians, they lived calm, peaceful, and spiritual lives. However, when acorns and other edible wild plants were ready for harvest, they worked hard to obtain the food they needed.

Great Basin Ute

This structure, known as a wickiup, was home to a Ute chief around 1873. The Ute lived in the mountains of Utah, Colorado, and New Mexico, where there were plenty of natural resources. They were on the move for most of the year but gathered in large groups in the summer.

▲ In this Pomo village, women grind acorns for food under the shelter of buildings made of branches and grass.

A variety of diets and homes

Tribes of the Great Basin lived in small family groups that moved from place to place. They ate mostly pine nuts, acorns, rabbits, insects, and birds. Plateau Indians ate mostly fish, roots, and berries. They lived in homes made of saplings covered with reeds. In the winter, they built their homes over an underground pit for warmth.

Peaceful and settled

When Europeans arrived in the late 1500s, California and the Northwest were more densely populated by American Indians than any other region north of Mexico. In California alone, it is estimated that about 300,000 people lived in 500 different villages. Except for a few villages that bordered hostile tribes, they were the only American Indians that never went to war. They did not need to fight, because they had what they needed to live peaceful lives.

◀ Baskets woven by the Nootka people of the Pacific Northwest

15

European Conquest
Explorers, invaders, and colonists

Europeans came to the New World looking for gold, opportunity, religious freedom, and to save the natives' souls. Their coming would change American cultures and lifestyles forever.

▲ Columbus steps ashore.

Although Vikings settled for a time along the coast of Newfoundland, Canada, around A.D. 1000, the real beginning of European conquest in the New World came in 1492, when Christopher Columbus and his men landed on the Caribbean island of Hispaniola (present-day Haiti and Dominican Republic).

Columbus was Italian, but his expedition was paid for by the royal family of Spain, and the Spanish became the first Europeans to explore and settle the New World. Columbus believed he had found a new route to India, so he called the native people Indians. We now refer to them as American Indians.

Jamestown Colony
In May 1607, 104 English colonists established Jamestown on an island in the James River in what is now Virginia. They built a wooden fort to protect them from the Indians, with several houses inside the walls.

The Conquest of Mexico
In 1519, the Spanish conquistador Hernando Cortés and his army invaded Mexico. Within two years, they had conquered the once-powerful Aztec Empire. The Aztec capital of Tenochtitlán, renamed Mexico City, became the base for further Spanish invasions.

▼ In the relentless search for gold, the Spanish attacked Indian towns and cities in Central America. With metal armor, guns, and horses, the invaders had a great advantage in warfare.

Horses, guns, and diseases

On their early New World expeditions, the Spanish brought horses. By 1650, Spanish ranchers had large herds in the Rio Grande valley of New Mexico, with Pueblo Indians helping them. Pueblo herdsmen often escaped their masters to join nearby tribes, taking Spanish horses with them and beginning the horse culture of the Plains Indians.

By 1770, horses had spread through the Great Plains, Columbia Plateau, and Rocky Mountains. The Europeans also brought gunpowder, guns, and other metal weapons, which the Indians used for hunting and warfare. The French, in particular, exchanged guns for valuable furs with the Indians. This angered the English and Spanish colonists.

But the most deadly introductions were European diseases, which wiped out whole tribes because the Indians had not developed immunity to them.

Jamestown Massacre, 1622

The English colonists and the Indians of the Powhatan Confederacy kept an uneasy peace for almost 15 years, until the English executed an Indian for suspected murder. On March 22, 1622, Powhatan warriors took revenge, killing 347 English colonists.

▼ French explorer Robert de La Salle visited the Caddo Indians in eastern Texas in May 1686.

▼ Spaniards traded trinkets for gold with the Taíno Indians of Hispaniola.

The Fur Trade

Although Spanish explorers and conquistadors did find gold and silver in Mexico, the most important early trade item in North America was the beaver pelt, which was highly valuable in Europe. Trading for beaver took place mainly in the Great Lakes region and later in the Rockies.

◀ Spanish halberds—weapons with an ax blade and spike at the end of a long pole

17

Changes on the Plains
The buffalo culture develops and spreads

For Plains Indians, buffalo herds provided almost everything they needed to live. Once they had horses, the people could follow the herds over great distances, carrying their homes and belongings with them.

Before they obtained horses, most Plains tribes lived in permanent or semipermanent villages near the Missouri River or the Rocky Mountains. There they farmed, hunted small game, and only once or twice a year ventured onto the treeless Great Plains to hunt buffalo.

Hunting on foot was difficult, and the men usually worked together to drive the beasts over a cliff. With only dogs to pull their belongings, they could not travel quickly or far from home. With horses, they could swoop close to the buffalo to shoot their bows and arrows and ride away quickly if a buffalo attacked. The horse also allowed them to carry tepees and their equipment. Some tribes became nomads, constantly traveling to follow the herds and good weather.

▲ The sun dance was the great religious ritual of the Plains Indians.

An Endless Resource
The buffalo, or American bison, once roamed from the Rocky Mountains to the East Coast. By 1800, the eastern herds had been killed off, but there were still about 50 million buffalo on the prairies and plains west of the Mississippi. For Plains Indians, the herds provided everything they needed to live.

▲ Traditional beaded moccasins made by the Sioux

▼ Although safer than hunting on foot, hunting buffalo on horseback could be dangerous.

18

Family Life

The Plains Indians maintained close family relationships whether they lived in permanent villages or traveled across the plains. Many members of an extended family might all live together in one large tepee.

▼ Men discuss plans for a hunt, war party, or move, while women make food and look after the children.

Made from Buffalo

Buffalo meat provided food. The hides were used for tepees, clothing, shields, and drums. The horns were turned into spoons, and bones were carved into tools. The stomach was used for a cooking pot, and the dung was burned as fuel when there was no wood.

Conflict between tribes

Before 1820, white settlers had made little impact on the Plains Indians. However, tribes regularly pushed one another out of their homelands through warfare. For example, in the 1600s, the Sioux, who later became the most powerful Indian nation in fighting the whites, were pushed out of their villages in eastern Minnesota by the Ojibwa and Cree tribes. The westernmost Sioux tribe, the Lakota, later developed the classic nomadic buffalo culture in the western Dakotas.

Farther west, the Comanche pushed the Apache southward into present-day New Mexico and Arizona and took over their lands on the southwestern plains.

◄ A rattle, skull, shield, and hide made from a buffalo

Indian Removal
Forced into conflict with whites

After the Revolutionary War of 1775 to 1781, white Americans began settling the forested lands west of the Appalachian Mountains. They battled the Indians who already lived there and decided to "remove" them west of the Mississippi River.

As Americans pushed west, they faced powerful Eastern Woodland and Southeastern tribes who claimed ownership of their traditional lands and were willing to fight for them. In the Great Lakes region, an Indian confederacy under the Miami leader Little Turtle crushed a white army in 1791 only to suffer a defeat three years later that forced them to give up a large area of present-day Ohio. In 1811, a confederacy under the Shawnee leader Tecumseh was defeated in what is now Indiana. By this time, the United States had obtained vast lands west of the Mississippi in the Louisiana Purchase (1803), and a plan had developed to move all the eastern Indians west of the river.

▲ William Penn made a treaty with the Delaware tribe in 1682 to establish the colony of Pennsylvania.

Signing Treaties
The first treaty between the U.S. government and the American Indians was signed with the Delaware tribe in 1780. During the next 91 years, some 800 treaties were signed with the Indians, and about half of those were made official by Congress. The treaties were supposed to be agreements between two equal sides, but as the United States grew stronger, it often broke its treaties.

▼ Despite relying on their support during the Creek War, General Andrew Jackson demanded that the Cherokee give up huge areas of land after the war was over.

▼ Major Stephen Long meets with the Pawnee in 1820 during his expedition to the Rocky Mountains.

Choosing Sides
The American Revolution split the Iroquois Confederacy, with four tribes fighting for the British and two siding with the Americans. During the War of 1812, Tecumseh died fighting for the British in Canada. In the South, the Cherokee, Choctaw, and some Creeks helped the Americans fight Creeks who supported the British.

The Indian Removal Act of 1830

U.S. explorers of the early 1800s, Zebulon Pike and Stephen Long, described the land we now call the Great Plains as a "desert" unsuitable for farming. As a result, U.S. leaders decided the land would be a good home for the American Indians who stood in the way of settlement east of the Mississippi. The Indian Removal Act of 1830 gave President Andrew Jackson authority to negotiate with tribes to move west of the Mississippi.

Five Civilized Tribes

White Americans called the Cherokee, Chickasaw, Choctaw, Creek, and Seminole the "Five Civilized Tribes" because they combined Indian and white cultures. Cherokee silversmith Sequoyah developed the first American Indian alphabet.

Fighting back

Even before the Indian Removal Act, some eastern tribes accepted new lands to the west. After the act, other tribes also accepted removal, no matter how painful. Some decided to fight. In 1832, the Sauk and Fox tribes fought in Illinois and Wisconsin under a leader named Black Hawk. In Florida, the Seminole fought from 1835 to 1842, and one U.S. Army soldier died for every two Seminoles who moved west.

◀ Out of 18,000 Cherokee who followed the Trail of Tears, about 4,000 died.

Trail of Tears

Between 1831 and 1859, the Five Civilized Tribes were forced to leave their homelands in the Southeast and move to a new "Indian Territory" in what is now Oklahoma. Although all the tribes suffered horribly on the journey, the Choctaw and Cherokee had the worst experiences, losing many thousands along the way. Both tribes call these journeys the Trail of Tears.

Making Treaties
New pressures after the Removal Act

As Indians were being removed west of the Mississippi, white settlers were crossing the Great Plains in search of California gold and the rich farmlands of Oregon.

Indian Treaty

As tension mounted along the westward trails, the U.S. government signed a treaty with Plains tribes at Fort Laramie (Wyoming) in 1851. The Indians promised that they would let travelers pass safely— and at first they did.

As soon as whites realized that the prairies just across the Mississippi River were ideal for farming, they wanted those Indian lands, too. The first white settlement in the current state of Iowa was established on land purchased from Black Hawk and his people in 1832, just two years after they had been granted the land in the treaty that ended the Black Hawk War.

The Oregon and California trails

In 1841, the first wagon train headed across the Great Plains to Oregon, drawn by reports of a fertile land and mild climate. Seven years later, the discovery of gold in California sparked tens of thousands of gold seekers to travel a similar route. For the first time, the Plains Indians realized that the whites might threaten their way of life.

▼ Indian tribes fought one another as well as settlers for buffalo hunting grounds.

Battles with Settlers

In the treaty of 1851, the U.S. government promised that the northern plains would belong to the Indians forever. In 1854, the territories of Kansas and Nebraska—in the heart of the plains—were opened for white settlement. As settlers moved west, conflicts began between whites and Indians over land promised in the treaty.

▲ Oglala Sioux chief wearing a bone breastplate, 1899

Warriors of Plains tribes that fought settlers

Indian attacks

At first the Indians were cautious, waiting to see what would happen as the whites traveled through their lands. Then, in 1847, the Cayuse—a Columbia Plateau tribe of eastern Washington—lost half their tribe to measles. They rightly believed that the disease had been passed to them by travelers who stopped at a mission on Cayuse land. In November 1847, the Cayuse attacked the mission and killed 14 whites.

Seven years later, in 1854, a conflict developed near Fort Laramie, in present-day Wyoming, when a hungry Lakota Sioux warrior killed an old, lame cow that had wandered into the Indian camp. The warrior shared the meat with his people. When the owner of the cow complained, the U.S. Army sent 30 soldiers to the camp to arrest the warrior. A fight broke out and every soldier was killed, beginning 36 years of conflict with the Sioux.

New Weapons

Eastern Indians obtained guns and other metal weapons from French and British traders during the 1600s. The Plains Indians, living farther from the whites, did not obtain these weapons until the late 1700s. It was not until the mid-1800s that guns were common. Since these guns allowed only one shot at a time, they were used for warfare more than buffalo hunting.

▲ Cheyenne warrior with a coup stick—a long curved pole used to touch an enemy as a sign of bravery

▲ ▶ Decorated rifle and metal tomahawk, obtained from white traders around 1870

23

The Conflict Explodes
Broken treaties lead to warfare

Throughout the West, pressure from white settlement, gold discoveries, and railroad building led to bloody conflicts between settlers and soldiers and the Indians whose traditional ways of life were threatened by these events.

From 1855 to 1861, conflicts between whites and Indians exploded in California, the Pacific Northwest, and the Southwest. In 1862, an uprising in Minnesota by eastern Sioux, called the Santee, left from 500 to 800 settlers and soldiers dead and brought the Lakota, who lived on the western plains, into the conflict.

Now the plains became the center of conflict, and the U.S. Army built forts throughout the region. From 1866 to 1868, a Lakota leader named Red Cloud led such strong resistance to a series of forts built in Montana to protect gold miners that the forts were abandoned. Peace was made, but it lasted only a few years.

▲ A Nez Perce warrior guards his people as they attempt to escape to Canada in 1877.

▼ Lakota Sioux warriors pillage a captured Union Pacific train in 1869.

▼ A surprise attack in November 1868 on a Cheyenne village on the Washita River in Oklahoma by the 7th U.S. Cavalry under Lieutenant Colonel George Custer

Sand Creek Massacre
In 1859, a gold discovery in Colorado brought around 100,000 white travelers across the plains. Four years later, warriors led by the Cheyenne began attacking travelers along the Platte River Road, shutting down the main trail to Colorado and the far West. Unable to battle the hostile warriors, Colorado volunteer soldiers attacked a peaceful Cheyenne village on Sand Creek, killing 300 men, women, and children.

Indians watched as settlers and prospectors moved into their territory—often breaking treaties as they were being written.

◀ White and Indian participants pose during the treaty negotiations at Fort Laramie in 1868.

▼ Soldiers, called bluecoats by the Indians (because of their uniforms), attacked Indian villages with deadly sabers.

Fort Laramie Treaty of 1868
To end the Red Cloud War, the U.S. government negotiated a new treaty with the Sioux and Arapaho at Fort Laramie in 1868. In return for peace, the government promised a huge "Great Sioux Reservation" —protected Indian land—that included the western half of what is now South Dakota.

War for the Black Hills
In 1874, Lieutenant Colonel George Custer led around 1,100 of his men into the Black Hills of western South Dakota—land that had been promised to the Indians in the 1868 Treaty of Fort Laramie. When Custer's men found gold there, thousands of white miners headed for the hills, sparking new conflicts. In late 1875, the U.S. War Department ordered all Indians of the Black Hills to leave that part of the Great Sioux Reservation by February 1, 1876, or they would be considered "hostile" and hunted down by soldiers.

The Little Bighorn
Many Lakota and Cheyenne would not give up that western part of the reservation. Led by Sitting Bull and Crazy Horse, they formed a large village, moving to hunt buffalo and antelope. Other Indians joined them until there were some 7,000 people and 1,800 warriors. On June 25, 1876, Custer, with 647 soldiers and scouts, attacked the village on the Little Bighorn River in Montana. He and 212 men under his immediate command were killed by the Indians.

After the Little Bighorn
The Battle of the Little Bighorn was the greatest victory of the American Indians over the U.S. Army—but it only strengthened the army's efforts to hunt them down. By 1877, Indian resistance on the plains had been overcome.

▶ Crazy Horse and Sitting Bull inspire their warriors at the Little Bighorn, June 25, 1876.

25

Reservations
The plight of Sitting Bull and Geronimo

In order to make room for white settlement, the U.S. government forced the Indians to move onto reservations—land reserved for them as part of their original lands or in other areas far from home.

▲ A Sioux burial platform. It became more difficult to maintain traditions on the reservation.

Indian reservations were established in the East beginning in 1758. After the Indian Removal Act of 1830, many more reservations were established west of the Mississippi. Some of these reservations were very large, but as pressure from white settlement continued, the government often broke its treaties and took more land.

Just a month after the Battle of the Little Bighorn, Lakota living on the eastern part of the Great Sioux Reservation were threatened with starvation unless they signed away their sacred Black Hills. It was sign or starve, and they signed. Later, in 1889, they were forced to give up much more of the reservation. Even worse than handing over land was the loss of their traditional way of life. After his surrender, Sitting Bull sang: "A warrior I have been. / Now it is all over. / A hard time I have."

Killing Buffalo

In 1870, a way was found to make fine leather from buffalo hides. White hunters slaughtered the beasts in massive numbers and shipped their hides east on the railroads. By 1889, less than 1,000 buffalo remained. Today there are about 30,000 in protected herds and almost 500,000 raised for meat on ranches.

▼ Cattle were brought from Texas to feed reservation Indians.

▼ Sitting Bull, his family, and a sympathetic white woman after his surrender

Sitting Bull

After the Battle of the Little Bighorn, Sitting Bull led his people into Canada. However, there were not enough buffalo to hunt, and early in 1881 he and his people returned. In July 1881, Sitting Bull and 187 followers surrendered to the U.S. Army in northern Dakota Territory.

◄ An Indian agent pays the trail boss for the cattle.

Sitting Bull joined Buffalo Bill's Wild West Show in 1885 for a tour of Canada. A photo of the two men together (below) was one of the most popular souvenirs.

Indian agencies

When Indians accepted a reservation, they were usually promised food and supplies. A government employee called an Indian agent was responsible for obtaining and distributing these goods—and for keeping an eye on the Indians. Although some agents cared about the Indians, most were only interested in making money for themselves.

In the Southwest, an Apache tribe called the Chiricahua were forced to live on the San Carlos Reservation in Arizona Territory. They hated this reservation, and groups escaped, terrorizing nearby ranches and towns. One leader, Geronimo, escaped four times with his followers before surrendering in September 1886. By that time, his people had been shipped to a military base in Florida. Geronimo and his band were sent to Florida, too.

Ghost Dance

In 1889, a Paiute Indian in Nevada named Wovoka began to preach a message of peace. He told his people to perform a traditional dance so they might be reunited with dead friends and relatives. This became known as the ghost dance. News spread throughout the West, and representatives of many tribes came to visit Wovoka.

◀ A buckskin "ghost shirt" with painted designs, made by an Arapaho Indian

▶ By dancing until exhausted, ghost dancers saw visions of the dead, the past, and—for some—a glorious future.

27

The Final Act
Wounded Knee and a new life

Although Wovoka preached "peace all over the world," the ghost dance became more warlike for the Lakota, who had just lost half their reservation. They believed their ghost shirts would stop white bullets and the dance would drive whites from their land.

In April 1890, two Lakota medicine men who had visited Wovoka established the ghost dance among their people. In October, Sitting Bull invited one of the medicine men, his nephew Kicking Bear, to teach the dance to the Indians near his home. The dance created fear among whites, and the Indian agent, John McLaughlin, sent Indian policemen—Sioux who worked with the whites—to arrest Sitting Bull. A fight broke out, and Sitting Bull was killed along with seven of his followers. Six policemen also died.

▲ The U.S. Army used four machine guns like this to mow down the Indians at Wounded Knee.

▼ It is unclear how the fighting began at Wounded Knee, but many of the dead Indians were women and children. Twenty-five soldiers also died.

Selling the Land
Land taken from the Indians was often sold by the government to white settlers. Although some tribes were supposed to receive payment when the land was sold, they seldom saw much of the money.

The Massacre at Wounded Knee
Survivors of Sitting Bull's camp joined a chief named Big Foot. He led his band on a 100-mile (160-km) flight to the South, where the 7th Cavalry forced them to camp on Wounded Knee Creek. Four army machine guns were set up above the camp. On December 29, the soldiers ordered the Lakota to give up their guns. The camp exploded in violence, and 146 Indians lay dead in the snow.

The frozen body of Chief Big Foot on the battlefield at Wounded Knee Creek in present-day South Dakota

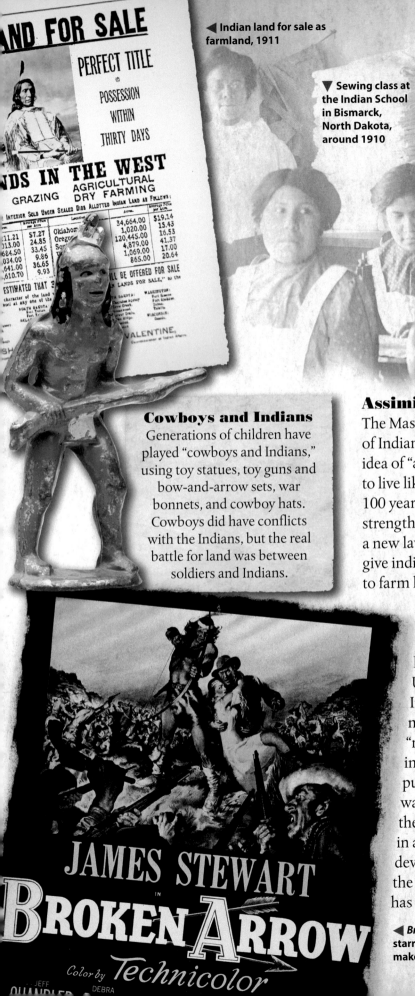

Indian land for sale as farmland, 1911

Sewing class at the Indian School in Bismarck, North Dakota, around 1910

LAND FOR SALE

PERFECT TITLE
POSSESSION
WITHIN
THIRTY DAYS

NDS IN THE WEST

GRAZING | AGRICULTURAL
DRY FARMING

Cowboys and Indians

Generations of children have played "cowboys and Indians," using toy statues, toy guns and bow-and-arrow sets, war bonnets, and cowboy hats. Cowboys did have conflicts with the Indians, but the real battle for land was between soldiers and Indians.

Assimilation

The Massacre at Wounded Knee was the last gasp of Indian resistance in the United States. The idea of "assimilating" the Indians—teaching them to live like whites—had been a goal for more than 100 years, but it took on stronger focus as the strength of the Plains tribes was broken. In 1887, a new law had allowed the U.S. government to give individual Indians areas of their reservations to farm like white settlers. Some were successful with this new life, but many struggled to survive in the white man's world.

Fact or fiction?

Until the 1960s, the image of American Indians in books, magazines, plays, and movies was one of two stereotypes: "noble savages"—simple people who lived in an untouched world of beauty and purity; or "bloodthirsty savages"—ruthless warriors who killed without mercy. In fact, the Indians were complex people who lived in a spiritual world, valued family, and developed a wide variety of cultures. Over the past 50 years, the white view of Indians has become more realistic.

JAMES STEWART

BROKEN ARROW

Color by Technicolor

Broken Arrow is a western movie made in 1950 starring James Stewart as Tom Jeffords, who tries to make peace between settlers and Apaches.

29

Glossary

adobe a brick made of mostly sand, clay, and water, dried in the sun

Anasazi ancestors of the Pueblo Indians who lived in apartment-style dwellings

band a group of Indians who live and travel together, usually with a leader

buckskin leather made from the skin of a male deer

civilized living according to the standards of the Europeans and Americans

confederacy a group of tribes who have agreed to keep peace with one another and fight together against their enemies

Congress part of the U.S. government in which representatives make laws

conquistador Spanish word meaning "conqueror"

council a group of people who meet to make decisions

culture a way of life for a group of people

customs special ways of doing things

extended family parents, children, aunts, uncles, and grandparents living together

fertile soil rich in nutrients, good for growing crops

Folsom culture hunters who lived around 9,000 to 10,500 years ago

hide the skin of an animal

immunity the ability of a body to fight off a disease, developed through previous contact with the disease

medicine man a term that whites applied to Indian spiritual leaders

mission a settlement set up by a church to convert local people to its faith

New World North and South America, as opposed to the Old World of Europe, Asia, and Africa

nomads people who do not have a fixed home and move from place to place

pelt the skin and fur of an animal

removal forcing people from their land

ritual an action, prayer, song, or other practice that has special meaning for a group of people

scalp the skin and hair cut from the top of the head

settlers people from distant lands who set up their home in a particular place

Sioux an Indian nation divided into seven tribes, including the Lakota; they lived mainly in what is now the western Dakotas and western Nebraska

stereotype a simple and often inaccurate image of how a person, group, or place probably behaves, lives, or looks

tepee a cone-shaped dwelling made of wooden poles and animal hide (skin), usually buffalo, that could be easily moved from place to place

totem pole in Northwest Indian cultures, a pole containing carved images of "totems"—animals or objects that have special power or meaning to the people

treaty an agreement between two or more nations or peoples

trinkets small items, often shiny and pretty, that have no real value

Vikings people from present-day Scandinavia (Norway, Sweden, and Denmark) who explored, raided, and settled throughout Europe and the North Atlantic islands from the late 700s to 1100s

whites Americans with light-colored skin whose families came from Europe

Timeline

1492 Christopher Columbus discovers America and meets the Taíno Indians of Hispaniola

1521 Spanish conquistador Hernando Cortés conquers the Aztec Empire in Mexico

1540 Spanish conquistador Francisco Coronado attacks Pueblo villages in modern-day New Mexico

1607 The first permanent English settlement in North America established at Jamestown, Virginia

1686 French explorer Robert de La Salle meets the Caddo Indians of Texas

1754–1763 Indians fight for both British and French during the French and Indian War

1789 The U.S. Constitution gives the federal government power to negotiate with Indian tribes

1794 An Indian confederacy under Little Turtle is defeated by white soldiers in present-day Ohio

1803 The Louisiana Purchase makes vast lands west of the Mississippi River part of the United States

1830 The Indian Removal Act

1847 Cayuse Indians kill 14 whites at the Whitman Mission on the Oregon Trail

1851 The first Treaty of Fort Laramie between northern Plains tribes and the U.S. government

1854 Hostilities begin between the Lakota Sioux and the U.S. government

1868 New treaties signed at Fort Laramie with the Sioux, Cheyenne, and Arapaho

1874 Discovery of gold in the Black Hills on land that was promised to the Indians at Fort Laramie

1876 Battle of the Little Bighorn

1876–1877 Most Lakota and Cheyenne accept reservation life, while Sitting Bull and his followers flee to Canada

1881 Sitting Bull and 187 followers surrender at Fort Buford in present-day North Dakota

1886 Apache leader Geronimo surrenders

1889 A large part of present-day Oklahoma is opened to white settlement

1890 The massacre of Lakota at Wounded Knee

Information

WEBSITES

Native American Facts for Kids
www.native-languages.org/kids.htm

School projects about American Indians
www.greatdreams.com/native.htm

Cahokia Mounds
www.cahokiamounds.org

Great Serpent Mound
www.highlandssanctuary.org

National Parks Service specific locations
www.nps.gov/chcu Chaco Culture site
www.nps.gov/colo Colonial sites: Jamestown
www.nps.gov/fola Fort Laramie
www.nps.gov/libi Little Bighorn Battlefield
www.nps.gov/meve Mesa Verde
www.nps.gov/whmi Whitman Mission

BOOKS TO READ

Gibson, Karen Bush. *Native American History for Kids: With 21 Activities.* Chicago, IL: Chicago Review Press, 2010.

Isaacs, Sally Senzall. *America in the Time of Sitting Bull: 1840 to 1890.* Des Plaines, IL: Heinemann Library, 2000.

Murdoch, David Hamilton, and Lynton Gardiner. *North American Indian.* DK Eyewitness Books. New York: DK, in association with the American Museum of Natural History, 2005.

Ostler, Jeffrey. *The Lakotas and the Black Hills: The Struggle for Sacred Ground.* New York: Viking, 2010.

Turner, Ann Warren, and Wendell Minor. *Sitting Bull Remembers.* New York: HarperCollins Publishers, 2007.

Walker, Paul Robert. *Remember Little Bighorn: Indians, Soldiers, and Scouts Tell Their Stories.* Washington, DC: National Geographic, 2006.

Index